PORTRAITS
of
TROPICAL
BIRDS

PORTRAITS
of
TROPICAL
BIRDS

By JOHN S. DUNNING

Field Collaborator, Cornell Laboratory of Ornithology

Research Associate, The Florida State University

LIVINGSTON PUBLISHING COMPANY

Wynnewood, Pennsylvania, 1970

Printed in the Netherlands
ISBN 0-87098-033-5

Library of Congress Catalog Card Number 71-134304

*Dedicated to my wife and to the memory of
my parents, who encouraged my love of nature
from earliest childhood*

Contents

Foreword

O N his retirement from business in Connecticut, John S. Dunning set for himself a singular goal: to photograph, close up and under uniform, true-to-life conditions, as many neotropical birds as time and effort allowed. How well he has achieved his objective so far is eloquently demonstrated in this handsome volume.

Turn the pages slowly, savoring each dazzling portrait—the subject fresh from its habitat and vibrant, eyes sparkling, stance alert. Note the consistency in portraiture. Each bird, without exception, is similarly and brilliantly lighted, revealing the many delicacies of feathering and the bold colors and subtle tints of the fleshy parts—the bill, eyes, eyelids, legs, feet, and other normally unfeathered areas.

Mr. Dunning tells in step-by-step detail how he caught his wild subjects, held them briefly, and took these superb photographs. And he acknowledges right away that always at his side, as aide and companion, was Harriet Dunning, his charming wife. Indeed, what we see in this book represents teamwork, the mutual dedication of two people to an exacting, arduous project.

Purists who consider as acceptable only photographs of birds living free in their natural environment might object to the portraits as "an easy way out" of getting real wildlife shots. But all of us must look at the pictures for what they are and recognize their truly great significance.

In their striking clarity, the photographs are as much a scientific record of each species as the actual specimens labelled and preserved in museum collections, and the descriptions written by the persons who originally identified and named the species. Besides showing the colors of the fleshy parts that dead specimens almost immediately lose, the pictures provide other complementary information about head crests, facial expressions, and body contours. Moreover, the photographs reveal the inadequacy of both preserved specimens and verbal descriptions in fully designating species. If the scientific records of all species could be accompanied by photographs of this quality for comparative purposes, imagine the aid such photographs would be to taxonomists in solving many of the puzzling relationships.

The photographs are firsts for many of the species. One—that of the hummingbird called Colorful Puff-leg—was taken in Colombia before the species was even known to science. When the Dunnings first netted this bird, conspicuously marked with a glittering cap, they could not identify it; it matched no published description of a species in Colombia. On the chance that it might be at least unusual, if not a new species, they brought the specimen home and later showed it to a recognized authority on Colombian birds, R. Meyer de Schauensee. Sure enough, the bird was a new species which Mr. de Schauensee later described and named *Eriocnemis mirabilis*.

The text accompanying most of the photographs is necessarily brief, not from lack of space but lack of information; in some instances, it constitutes the sum total of our knowledge of the species. Such matters as the role of the bird in its environment, its repertoire of behaviors including song and calls, its food, and its nesting habits are not mentioned for the simple reason that they have not been reported. Even the nests of some species remain undiscovered. Lest there be persons inclined to view ornithology as an exhausted science, may I call their attention to this bird-rich part of the world where the Dunnings have been, where ornithology is still in its infancy, literally awaiting practitioners.

When turning the pages, keep constantly in mind that many of the species portrayed are sharply restricted to particular—usually forested—habitats, now being depleted at an alarmingly accelerated rate. This suggests the distressing possibility that some of the species, since they are almost certainly incapable of accepting new habitats once they lose those to which they are stringently adapted, may soon disappear forever should their habitats be entirely eliminated. Horrible as the thought may be, the photographs of certain species in this book could very well be the last ever taken.

We are grateful to the Dunnings. In these pages they give us the joy of seeing neotropical birds in all their pristine beauty. More importantly, they provide a reminder, impressive and timely, that here in a sense are creatures begging for attention—from ornithologists to study their ways of life and from conservationists (meaning all of us!) to stem their trend to oblivion.

OLIN SEWALL PETTINGILL, JR.

Introduction

To the legion of birdwatchers looking for new fields to conquer—new names to put on the life list—the American tropics have much to offer. Starting at the southern borders of the United States and stretching from Mexico to Bolivia lies the richest birding area in all the world.

The country of Colombia, for instance, has over twice as many species of birds as the continental United States though it is only one-seventh the size. This is partly because of the wide diversity of habitats, from the tropical lowland jungles to the arctic zones high up in the Andes Mountains. Another reason is that many specialized forms of bird life can only develop in the tropics, with their uniform habitat the year round.

Tropical birds with highly specialized bills that give them an advantage in obtaining a certain food in the fiercely competitive world of nature could never live through a northern winter. Snow and cold might eliminate completely the small ecological niche which they have learned to exploit and on which their lives depend.

Some birds solve this problem by migrating; indeed, a number of the birds which we in the United States enjoy seeing and hearing during spring and summer spend a good part of the year in the tropics. But migration is a very hazardous undertaking—one to be avoided if at all possible—and its dangers are probably the main reason that most migrating birds lay four or more eggs at each nesting, while most nonmigratory species of perching birds appear to be able to maintain their populations with but two eggs per clutch.

My wife and I were first exposed to the wonderfully diverse bird life of the tropics when we took a trip with the Florida Audubon Society to Central America. Every day we saw new birds—some with the huge bills of the toucans, some having small bills like the manakins, and in between the spadebills, the scythebills, the sicklebills. "Bird fever" struck me for the second time! The first attack had come many years before, when my eyes were first opened to the feathered beauties of the Connecticut countryside where I was fortunate to spend my boyhood. Only those who have been so stricken can understand the intensity of "bird fever."

This second attack of it came at a time when it seemed that I might at last indulge a lifelong dream of spending full time in the world of nature. Until then the demands of raising and educating five children had made it impossible. But now they were all on their own. And my wife was willing to try it with me. How lucky I was!

At this opportune time, a friend told of hearing about some extensive bird-banding work in Panama. The birds were captured in a mist net, a lightweight numbered aluminum band was attached to one leg, and then the bird was released. When the bird was recaptured, its age, wanderings, and so on could be determined. Our knowledge of birds is being greatly extended by such studies.

Many interesting plumage variations in the birds were turning up in the Panama banding program. The director, Dr. Horace Loftin, thought that a photographic record of such plumages would be worthwhile. In addition, good color pictures would add to the scientific knowledge of "soft-part colors" (eyes, legs, bills), which fade in museum skins and thus are not available for researchers and illustrators.

Soon we were in Panama, little knowing how unprepared we were to make such a photographic record. I remember so well our first morning out with the bird banders. A bird was handed to us. We did the only thing we could do—my wife held the bird in her hand while I focused the camera on it. The results were awful. The bird was scared and looked it. The legs did not show. The lighting in the forest was inadequate.

We knew we must find a better way.

We had so much to learn. How could we get the bird to appear natural? How could we get enough light to show details? Did the bird prefer a perch that was horizontal, slanting, or vertical, small or large, moss-covered, leafy, or bare, with or without ants (almost every tree in the tropics has some ants), firm or springy? Did the bird stay mostly on the ground, in brush, or up in the trees? Where could we find photographic equipment which could stand the constant humidity of the rain forest, where our clothing mildewed and nothing ever seemed to dry out? And how could we accomplish all that and still keep our equipment light enough to carry through the jungle, convenient enough to erect quickly, and simple enough to be reliable?

It took about two years of trial and error. We still make changes but now they are minor. Details of our present equipment are discussed at the end of the book.

Photographing birds in an enclosure after capturing them in a mist net has some important advantages. In the first place, it makes it unnecessary to work around the bird's nest, which involves more or less unavoidable danger to the young. Photographing birds in juvenal or changing plumages, which would be very difficult by any other method, becomes possible. Pictures of birds which would seldom even be seen in the dense foliage of the tropics can be obtained. Frequently we work for several days in an area without ever seeing in the wild some of the species which quite commonly get into the nets. This is particularly true of birds which stay near the ground.

Birds photographed by this method have been living on natural food and thus their colors are quite normal, unlike those of the artificially fed birds in a zoo. Most important of all, after a brief period in the enclosure, the bird is released unharmed to resume its normal life in its own familiar habitat.

Placing the nets so as to get the birds we want is a particular problem—especially for the treetop birds. We have tried many schemes for mounting nets high up in the forest. Except for a few special situations, all have been abandoned—despite our frustration at seeing much-wanted birds fly over our nets. The work and time involved were just too great. It is my present opinion that *all* birds do, at times, come close to the ground and that study and work on netting them at those times are more productive than the large amount of time and effort necessary to erect high nets. This is especially true for us; since we spend only a few days to a week in any one spot, all our equipment must be very mobile.

Nets placed on the crest of a ridge will often capture high-flying birds going from the crown of a tree on one side of the ridge to a tree on the other side. A low food tree will sometimes lure them down. Best of all, perhaps, is a narrow neck of low woods connecting two substantial forest areas. At times the birds will pour through the narrow area to get from one forest to the other. This is particularly true of fruit eaters, which, I believe, travel long distances to get the ripening berries of certain trees.

When a bird flies into the net, the net "gives" as much as two or three feet, stopping the bird gently and dropping it into a pocket of the net. There the bird becomes entangled in the meshes. We try to release it as soon as possible so that the feathers will not become frayed by the bird's struggles.

Releasing birds from the net is an art at which my wife has become particularly adept; whenever I find a badly entangled bird, I always call her. The standard order is feet first, then wings, and last the head, but it is not always easy. Occasionally we are forced to cut the net to get the bird out quickly.

The next problem is mounting the correct perch and background foliage in the enclosure. After this the bird is put in and we try to get it to calm down and look natural. That is not as difficult as it sounds if quiet is maintained, though individual birds react as differently as individual people do. It helps to put some of the bird's favorite food in with it—we frequently have one feeding inside the enclosure. However, even when the bird calms down, it does not necessarily stay still, for that is not the nature of most birds. Quick focusing and tripping of the camera are necessary.

Any method of photographing birds provides a real challenge. It goes without saying that there will be many failures. That merely enhances the satisfaction when a slide comes back from the developer showing a well-posed bird in sharp focus with the proper lighting to show details.

The order of presentation of the plates and the English names used are substantially those in *The Species of Middle American Birds*, by Eugene Eisenmann, and *The Species of Birds of South America*, by Rodolphe Meyer de Schauensee. The approximate length of the bird is given in inches and the scientific name tells the genus and species. No mention is made of subspecific differences, which are usually slight. The birds shown on the plates are adult males unless otherwise noted.

How does one acknowledge the assistance of all who have helped along the way? It is clearly impossible and would be much too long to include here, anyway. Yet these pictures and this book could not have materialized without that help. I would like first to make mention of four whose help on our project was specially important:

Horace Loftin, on the staff of The Florida State University program in The Canal Zone, opened many doors and solved many problems in the early years of our effort. His assistance and encouragement at that time were instrumental in our getting started.

In the last three years, Kjell von Sneidern, Curator of the Natural History Museum of the University of Cauca in Popayan, Colombia, has organized camping expeditions into the jungles of that country which have resulted in photographs of a number of birds which are rare or hard to find. The difficulties of placing a net in a desirable spot never deterred Kjell. In all ways he did everything possible to get the maximum results for us.

Eugene Eisenmann, Research Associate of The American Museum of Natural History, gave unstintingly of his time in helpful criticisms, in working out identifications, and suggesting promising areas for our work in Panama.

Philip A. Livingston, with his great interest in tropical birds and his extensive knowledge of publishing, gave assistance which was very necessary and which few others could have given.

In addition to the above four, my deepest gratitude for advice, cooperation or assistance, large or small, goes to the following:

In the United States: William Belton, Department of State; E. Alexander Bergstrom, editor, *Bird Banding* magazine; Leslie Campbell, Belchertown, Mass.; Robert K. Godfrey, Robert Hull, Henry Stevenson of The Florida State University, Tallahassee; Howard S. Irwin, Head Curator, New York Botanical Garden; Douglas A. Lancaster, Cornell Laboratory of Ornithology; Thomas E. Lovejoy III, Peabody Museum, Yale University; C. Russell Mason and Nina Dean Steffee, Florida Audubon Society; R. Meyer de Schauensee, Academy of Natural Sciences of Philadelphia; Charles E. O'Brien, American Museum of Natural History; Alexander Wetmore and J. J. Wurdack, Smithsonian Institution; Carl Withner, Department of Biology, Brooklyn College, New York.

In The Canal Zone: Roy Sharp and Roy C. Zorn of the Canal Zone Administration.

In Colombia: F. Carlos Lehmann, Museo de Historia Natural, Cali; Antonio Olivares, Universidad Nacional de Colombia, Bogota.

In Venezuela: William Phelps and Paul Schwartz, Caracas.

On the book itself, the staff of Livingston Publishing Company very efficiently handled the many details, and their consultant Donald E. Cooke provided imaginative ideas on layout.

And finally my wife, Harriet, to whom this book is dedicated, has helped on every phase of the whole project in ways that every husband will understand. I could not have done it without her.

JOHN S. DUNNING

THE BIRDS

PLATE *1*

Family TROCHILIDAE:
Hummingbirds

The hummingbirds are a family of more than 300 small, brightly colored, active species found only in the New World and mainly in the tropics. The male's bright, iridescent colors and pugnacious nature and the swift, darting flight of both sexes make hummingbirds very conspicuous in flight. They have the unique ability to hover and fly backward as well as forward. They sip nectar from flowers and eat small insects. The females are usually plain-colored and raise the young without the help of the male.

The Lazuline Sabrewing is a hummingbird that inhabits forest and scrub areas. The shape of the leading feather on the wing gives it the name sabrewing. The history of the scientific name of this species illustrates the vagaries of our taxonomic methods—the Latin name given here is the ninth by which this species has been known.

Lazuline Sabrewing

Campylopterus falcatus

RANGE: Tropical and subtropical zones. Colombia, northern
Venezuela, and eastern Ecuador.
Length, 5½ inches

PLATE 2

Owing to the remoteness and limited extent of its known range, the Colorful Puff-leg had not been discovered before we photographed it in 1967. I observed a male feeding on low flowers in a small clearing at the edge of the woods and we caught several of them in our nets. All were released except one male that we collected. On a later trip we collected two more males, but other searchers have had difficulty locating any. The puffs of white feathers on the legs put this species into the group of hummingbirds known as puff-legs.

Colorful Puff-leg

Eriocnemis mirabilis

RANGE: Subtropical zone. Known only from one locality on
Charguayaco Mountain in the western Andes of Colombia.
Length, 4½ inches

PLATE 3

The Long-tailed Sylph is fairly common in forest and scrub on mountain slopes. It has two claims to distinction: it builds a domed nest—bulkier and less tidy than the compact cup of other hummingbirds—and it has glittering tail feathers which are unusual among hummingbirds. The male also has a glittering purple gorget and green crown, but try as I would I could not get them to show in the same photograph.

Long-tailed Sylph

Aglaiocercus kingi

RANGE: Tropical to temperate zones. Northern Venezuela and Colombia southward through Ecuador, eastern Peru, and northern Bolivia. Length, male, 5–8½; female, 4½ inches

PLATE 4

Family TROGONIDAE: Trogons

The trogons are among the world's most brilliantly colored birds. Of the 36 species in the world, 20 occur in Middle and South America, where their sonorous notes are distinctive sounds of the tropical forests. Except when feeding, they tend to sit quietly upright on a horizontal branch; they will allow a person to approach quite close before reluctantly fluttering to a nearby limb. Nests are made in cavities in dead trees or sometimes in termite nests. Trogon body feathers are exceedingly soft and silky and come out very easily—probably many a predator has caught a mouthful of feathers when trying for a meal of trogon.

Collared Trogon

Trogon collaris

RANGE: Tropical to montane zones from Mexico to Brazil and Bolivia.
Length, 9¾ inches

The Collared Trogon occurs on plantations and in forests at middle elevations. It often sits in one place for many minutes uttering a series of monotonous notes at intervals. As in other trogons, the female is much less colorful, usually a dull brown.

PLATE *5*

Black-throated Trogon

Trogon rufus

RANGE: Tropical zone. Southern Honduras south through South
America to southern Brazil, Paraguay, and northern Argentina.
Length, 9¾ inches

The Black-throated Trogon occurs in virgin forests, forest edge,
and sometimes in drier, more open woodland at lower
elevations than the Collared Trogon. It perches in the lower
branches or understory of the forest. When alarmed, it makes a
typical cackling or churring call, slowly raises its tail to an
almost upright position, and more rapidly lowers it. Trogons of
both sexes participate in nest building, incubation, and feeding
of the young. Digging with its bill, this species excavates a
shallow, unlined nest cavity 4 to 12 feet above the ground in a
well-decayed tree trunk. I observed this trogon feeding: it would
hover before a cluster of fruit, pick off the berries one by one,
and return to a nearby perch to swallow each berry.

PLATE **6**

Family ALCEDINIDAE: Kingfishers

Although kingfishers have worldwide distribution, most of the species in this large family are found in the Old World. Many live quite far from water and subsist on insects; others get their food by plunging for fish from a perch above water. Their large, sharp-edged bills are well adapted to holding a squirming fish. They nest in burrows in banks, cavities in trees, or sometimes in termite nests. Both parents incubate and care for the young.

The tiny Pygmy Kingfisher, about the size of a sparrow, prefers the shaded pools and small streams of the forest. Perched on a low limb, it teeters, as many other kingfishers do, catching small fish and flying insects with a quick, darting flight. Despite its fairly wide range, it does not seem to be really common anywhere.

Pygmy Kingfisher

Chloroceryle aenea

RANGE: Tropical zone. Southern Mexico south to Bolivia and southeast
Brazil.
Length, 5¼ inches

PLATE **7**

Family MOMOTIDAE: Motmots

The eight species of motmots, a tropical American family, are known for their beautiful plumage and the long racquet-type tails which adorn all but one member of the family. Generally solitary and rather sluggish in behavior, motmots have the habit of irregularly shifting their tails from side to side like the pendulum of an erratic clock. They feed on a variety of insects, fruits, and small animals and nest in crevices or burrows in banks.

Tody Motmot

Hylomanes momotula

RANGE: Tropical zone. Found discontinuously from southern Mexico to northwest Colombia.
Length, 7 inches

Smallest of all the motmots, the inconspicuous Tody Motmot is the only one which lacks the long racquet tail of other members of the family. It frequents the undergrowth of humid forests, where it feeds in typical motmot style, darting out from its perch to catch flying or stationary prey or to pluck small fruits from among the leaves. It also is known to eat eggs from other birds' nests. One observer often saw clay on the bill and stains on the tail of this species, probably from digging a burrow for its nest.

PLATE **8**

Broad-billed Motmot

Electron platyrhynchum

RANGE: Tropical zone. Honduras south to Ecuador west of the Andes and to Bolivia east of the Andes.
Length, 14 inches

The Broad-billed Motmot has the typically long motmot tail with racquetlike tips on the central feathers. When these feathers first grow they have a normal structure, but the barbs along a section of the shaft are loosely attached and come off with normal wear and preening. The function of these unusual tail feathers is not known. This species hunts in high shrubs and understory in the forest edge and second growth. Although its presence is made known by a call very like a snoring sound, this sound is difficult to trace to its source.

PLATE *9*

Family GALBULIDAE: Jacamars

Because of their brilliant and often metallic green plumage, their long, thin, straight bills, and their quick movements, the 15 species of jacamars are often compared to hummingbirds. This tropical American family is most abundant in the Amazon basin. Hunting from exposed perches in forest clearings or second growth, jacamars catch insects in flight, often large, conspicuous dragonflies, butterflies, and beetles. For their nests they dig burrows in banks, steep hillsides, mounds of dirt on the upturned roots of fallen trees, or—rarely—termite nests.

Both sexes of the Yellow-billed Jacamar are the same size, although here the male appears smaller because he is crouched down in front of the female. This species is mostly found in the lower trees and shrubbery of the hilly forests in its range.

Yellow-billed Jacamar

Galbula albirostris

Left: male   Right: female
RANGE: Tropical zone. From the Guianas and southern Venezuela
southward east of the Andes through Colombia, Ecuador, Amazonian
Brazil, and Peru.
Length, 8 inches

PLATE *10*

Rufous-tailed Jacamar

Galbula ruficauda

RANGE: Tropical zone. Southern Mexico southward through Colombia, Venezuela, and the Guianas to Paraguay and northeastern Argentina.
Length, 10¾ inches

The most widespread and familiar member of the jacamar family, the Rufous-tailed Jacamar, occurs in humid second growth and in rain forest. I watched this individual for some time at the edge of a clearing produced by a small landslide in the forest. It sat in typical jacamar fashion with its long, thin bill tilted upward, alertly turning its head from side to side. Every minute or so it made a swift foray to snap up an insect, returning to its perch to eat. Jacamars are often first noticed by the loud clicking sound the bird's bill makes as it captures an insect. They often beat their insect prey against the perch to kill it and to knock off the insect's wings before swallowing it. The burrow, which both sexes help dig, may be up to 1½ feet long.

PLATE **11**

Family BUCCONIDAE: Puffbirds

A chunky, apparently neckless bird on an exposed perch at the edge of the forest is likely to be one of the puffbirds. The 30 species are limited to the American tropics. Judging by their behavior as we handled them, I believe that the reason these birds puff out their feathers to look much larger than normal is to discourage predators. Most puffbirds also have a very unpleasant odor (and possibly taste), which probably helps protect them. Those that have been studied build their nests in cavities in trees, burrows in the ground, or in arboreal termite nests.

The Chestnut-capped Puffbird can be seen perched at the edge of the forest feeding rather like a flycatcher, darting out from a perch to snatch insects in the air. After catching an insect it often goes to a new perch, instead of returning to the one from which it flew, as most flycatchers do. The heavy, hooked bill of this species helps to hold the biggest prey. Its nesting habits are not known.

Chestnut-capped Puffbird

Bucco macrodactylus

RANGE: Tropical zone. Northern South America east of the Andes
south to Bolivia.
Length, 6½ inches

PLATE *12*

White-whiskered Puffbird

Malacoptila panamensis

RANGE: Tropical and subtropical zones. Southern Mexico to Ecuador.
Length, 8¼ inches

The White-whiskered Puffbird has been called stupid because it will allow people to approach so close. Found alone or in pairs in tangled thickets or forest understory, it usually sits silent and erect, occasionally flicking its tail upwards or sideways. Its diet of insects and spiders is varied with centipedes and small lizards that may be as long as the bird itself. This puffbird mainly catches prey from leaves, twigs, and branches, often beating it on a perch before eating it. The entrance to the nest, which is in a chamber at the end of a sloping tunnel that the pair digs in the forest floor, is hidden by a ring of dead leaves and twigs. The parents deliver food to their young at the mouth of the burrow.

PLATE *13*

Family CAPITONIDAE: Barbets

The 76 species of barbets are widely distributed in the tropical areas of the world. In form they are large-headed stocky birds with heavy, conical bills. Their diet may consist entirely of insects or fruits or a mixture of the two. Although barbets often sit motionless, they are sometimes active feeders. Their call is usually a monotonous series of notes. The pattern of the feet— two toes directed forward and two backward—shows that barbets, like the jacamars, puffbirds, and toucans, are related to the woodpeckers. Barbets nest in cavities in trees.

Scarlet-crowned Barbet

Capito aurovirens

Left: female   Right: male
RANGE: Tropical zone. East of the Andes in Colombia, Ecuador, Peru, and western Brazil.
Length, 7½ inches

The scarlet crown that gives this bird its name occurs on the male only, but the frosty white crown of the female is equally attractive. In January they seemed to be staying together in mated pairs. The feeding and nesting habits of this species are not known.

PLATE *14*

The Red-headed Barbet is usually seen in humid forest edge or second-growth areas as a member of a mixed flock of feeding birds. It feeds very actively, hopping, hanging, and stretching to examine leaves, twigs, and epiphytes for insects or fruit. It generally stays at or below medium heights and has not been heard making any call or note.

Red-headed Barbet

Eubucco bourcierii

RANGE: Subtropical zone. Costa Rica to western Venezuela and
southward to Peru.
Length, 6½ inches

PLATE **15**

Family RAMPHASTIDAE: Toucans

The 37 species of toucans are well known for their enormous and colorful bills. Extremely light and strong, these bills are very effective for reaching and breaking open the fruits which form a major part of the toucan's diet. The bird also takes insects, spiders, and even the eggs or young of other birds. The unusual bristle-edged tongue is difficult to explain—possibly it helps in extracting the pulp of fruits. Toucans usually travel in noisy flocks in the tops of the trees. They roost and nest in cavities in trees.

Generally living at higher altitudes than the others, toucanets are the smallest members of the Toucan family. We have observed them prowling low in the forest more than their larger relatives do. Toucanets are greatly feared by small birds because of their habit of robbing nests. They move up and down the mountains with the wet and dry seasons. (The detailed photograph below is of a different bird.)

Crimson-rumped Toucanet

Aulacorhynchus haematopygius

RANGE: Upper tropical and subtropical zones. Andes of Venezuela,
Colombia, and Ecuador.
Length, 16 inches

PLATE **16**

Family PICIDAE: Woodpeckers

The more than 200 species of woodpeckers occur almost throughout the world. Most members of this family are especially adapted to a life on the trunks of trees, with strong feet and sharp curved nails for clinging to bark, stiffened tail feathers for extra support, a sharp bill for drilling wood, and an unusually long bristle-tipped tongue for extracting grubs from tunnels. Their distinctive undulating flight is easily recognized. Like their close relatives, the barbets, jacamars, puffbirds, and toucans, they have two toes forward and two back (most birds have three toes forward and only one back).

Golden-olive Woodpecker

Piculus rubiginosus

RANGE: Subtropical and upper tropical zones. Mexico southward to Brazil, Bolivia, and Argentina.
Length, 8½ inches

The Golden-olive Woodpecker, a fairly common species, is found alone or in pairs and prefers semiopen areas. In the few cases of nesting that have been described, the cavity used by the female for roosting becomes the nest site. As he was climbing the limb, this male vented his displeasure at being in the photographic enclosure by giving the limb a vicious whack with his sharp bill, breaking off the large chip shown near his tail.

PLATE **17**

Family DENDROCOLAPTIDAE: Woodcreepers

Restricted to the New World tropics, the woodcreepers form a quite uniform family of brownish birds. They live on tree trunks and branches and have stiffened tails like the unrelated woodpeckers. The bills of the approximately 50 species vary from short and straight to long and curved and are used for probing and prying for insect food. Species which have been studied nest in cavities, old woodpecker holes, and hollow stumps.

The Red-billed Scythebill, a rather uncommon bird, uses its amazing decurved bill for probing into such places as the bases of palm leaves, the centers of palm fruit clusters, the crevices of furrowed bark, the bases of epiphytes, and the tangles of tightly wound woody vines. Its call is a melodious rising and falling series of notes.

Red-billed Scythebill
Campylorhamphus trochilirostris

RANGE: Tropical and subtropical zones. Central Panama south through
northern South America to Peru and Paraguay.
Length, 9½ inches

35

PLATE *18*

Family FURNARIIDAE: Ovenbirds

The ovenbirds form a large American family of over 200 extremely diverse species which range throughout Central and South America in almost every type of habitat. Adaptation to these varied conditions has produced birds which forage in many different ways and build a great variety of nests—the domed ovenlike structures of mud which some of them build give the family its common name.

The protruding spines on the tail of the Pearled Treerunner are soft and not regularly used for support in climbing. This forest-dwelling bird is more likely to be seen searching for insects on small twigs and branches than on the trunks of trees. Its movements are fast and jerky, and it generally flies only a short distance at a time.

Pearled Treerunner
Margarornis squamigera
RANGE: Tropical through temperate zones. The Andes from Venezuela
southward through Bolivia.
Length, 6¼ inches

PLATE *19*

Family FORMICARIIDAE: Antbirds

The antbird family, confined to Central and South America, includes about 224 species of rather dull-plumaged birds. Species' common names, such as antwren, antshrike, and antpitta, indicate what sort of bird each is supposed to resemble. They are heard more often than seen because they tend to stay on or near the ground in brushy areas. Nests too are usually near or on the ground. The family takes its name from the habit that many (but by no means all) antbirds have of following swarms of foraging army ants—not to eat the ants, but to capture the terrified insects which are flushed by the ants.

Found in dense thickets of the humid lowlands, usually in pairs, the heavy-bodied Great Antshrike uses its strong hooked bill to tear apart vegetation to get at the insects hidden inside. It is a watchful, noisy bird; when disturbed, the male may erect the feathers of his back, exposing their white bases. Both sexes sing the distinctive song of the species, help build the exceptionally bulky, open nest, and raise the young.

Great Antshrike

Taraba major

Left: male   Right: female
RANGE: Tropical zone. Southern Mexico south through Central and
South America to northern Argentina.
Length, 8¼ inches

PLATE *20*

Barred Antshrike

Thamnophilus doliatus

Above: male   Below: female

RANGE: Tropical and subtropical zones. Eastern Mexico south to
Bolivia and northeastern Argentina.
Length, 6½ inches

The Barred Antshrike, which despite its name seldom follows
army ants, is common and widespread in thickets and brushy
areas. It frequently approaches and, crest erected, chatters
at an intruder. Even so, it is often not seen because of the
dense foliage of its habitat. The distinctive song—a descending
series of notes of quickening pace ending with a vibrating
chatter—is sometimes sung in duet by both members of the
pair. The nest is a small cuplike structure in the fork of a
horizontal branch near the ground.

PLATE **21**

The antwrens are the smallest members of the family. They are active, noisy feeders in the understory, lower trees, and canopy of second-growth forest. They forage often in flocks of mixed species, gleaning insects from leaves and poking into epiphytes and snags. Both male and female often flick their tails open and closed, exposing the white spots in the tail. When in groups the Dot-winged Antwren sometimes engages in displays. The males spread their tails, half spread their wings and fluff the feathers of their upper backs to create white humps, which contrast with the dark plumage. They are found in pairs at all times of the year.

Dot-winged Antwren

Microrhopias quixensis

Female

RANGE: Tropical zone. Southern Mexico to Peru west of the Andes and
Bolivia and Brazil east of the Andes.
Length, 4½ inches

PLATE 22

The active Long-tailed Antbirds travel in pairs or small groups, sometimes with other species. Constantly chirping as they forage, they are often found in dense growths of fern but inhabit other types of second growth as well. The streaked portions of the female's plumage are rufous and black; of the male's white and black. This individual lived in a clearing in the rain forest at 7,500 feet above sea level in the Colombian Andes, well above the elevation at which army ants occur; obviously these birds must get their food in other ways. Their nesting habits are not known.

Long-tailed Antbird

Drymophila caudata

Female

RANGE: Upper tropical and subtropical zones. Slopes of mountains in
Venezuela, Colombia, eastern Peru, Ecuador, and northern Bolivia.
Length, 6½ inches

PLATE *23*

The White-plumed Antbird, true to its family name, follows swarms of army ants and captures the insects they flush, relying on these swarms of ants almost entirely for finding its food. It is often the most numerous species in the somewhat noisy flocks of 20 to 30 birds of many species that follow the ants through the undergrowth of the moist rain forest. Both the male and female have the distinctive "horns" formed of white feathers. Nothing is known about the nesting habits of this bird.

White-plumed Antbird

Pithys albifrons

RANGE: Tropical zone. Guianas and Venezuela southward east of the
Andes through Colombia, Ecuador, Amazonian Brazil, and Peru.
Length, 5½ inches

PLATE *24*

The Spotted Antbird bears out its family name—one of the best ways to locate an army ant swarm in this bird's range is to listen for its calls. Individuals or pairs may be found throughout the forest, but several pairs may appear at one ant swarm. Both sexes then become very excited and active. They flit from one vertical perch to another, revolve around a perch, or chase one another, spreading and flicking their tails continuously. A pursuing bird erects the chestnut feathers on its back to expose a white patch there. The male often feeds the female during courtship, and both sexes help build the nest, incubate the eggs, and feed the young.

Spotted Antbird

Hylophylax naevioides

RANGE: Tropical zones. Honduras to western Ecuador.
Length, 5¼ inches

PLATE **25**

The Ocellated Antbird is among the most consistent of the army ant followers. It dominates the smaller antbirds and other species at an ant swarm, chasing them away with a loud flurry of wings and the snapping of its bill. If other species are near it, it utters a grunting call. One observer noted a member of this species standing calmly while ants swarmed over its feet, indicating that the birds are not interested in the ants as food. The Ocellated Antbird constantly raises and lowers its tail—this photograph caught the bird holding the tail in its lowest position. The blue area around the eye is bare skin.

Ocellated Antbird

Phaenostictus mcleannani

RANGE: Tropical and lower subtropical zones. Southeastern Honduras
to northwestern Ecuador.
Length, 8½ inches

PLATE **26**

The Black-spotted Bare-eye lives in second-growth habitats, where it often feeds among foraging army ants. It will allow its mate to forage quite close but will chase away other individuals of its own and other species. Like the Ocellated Antbird (Plate 25), this bird has bare skin around the eye. It is tempting to speculate that this gives an advantage in feeding among army ants, but more study is needed before we can jump to that conclusion. The nesting habits of the Black-spotted Bare-eye are unknown.

Black-spotted Bare-eye

Phlegopsis nigromaculata

RANGE: Tropical zone. East of the Andes in Colombia, Ecuador, Peru,
northern Bolivia, and Amazonian Brazil.
Length, 7¼ inches

PLATE **27**

The antpittas form a distinctive group of antbirds adapted for terrestrial life in the rain forest. They are sparrow- to robin-sized birds with stocky bodies, long, strong legs, and ridiculously small tails. The sexes are more similar than in other antbirds. Because of their quiet and seclusive habits, antpittas are extremely difficult to watch. Little is known about the Rufous-crowned Antpitta, which has a limited range. Other antpittas of the same genus live alone or in pairs. As they walk along the forest floor, the members of a pair keep in contact with whistled call notes.

Rufous-crowned Antpitta

Pittasoma rufopileatum

RANGE: Tropical zone. Pacific slope of Colombia and Ecuador.
Length, 7 inches

PLATE *28*

Family COTINGIDAE: Cotingas

The cotingas, a large (88 species), exclusively American family, contain some of the most striking of all tropical birds—as well as many that are dull and nondescript. Though very diverse, they are classed together because of a combination of anatomical features involving the structure of their vocal organs and that of their legs and feet. Since the cotingas generally live in or near the canopy of the forest, where they are hard to observe, little is known about most of the species.

Green-and-black Fruiteater

Pipreola riefferii

RANGE: Upper tropical to lower temperate zones. Venezuela south through the Andes of Colombia, Ecuador, and northern Peru.
Length, 7¾ inches

The Green-and-black Fruiteater plucks fruits and insects from treetop branches, often while hovering in the manner of a trogon. This cotinga is very well camouflaged as it sits quietly on a branch in the upperstory of the forest. It is fairly common in the forested mountains above the Cauca valley in Colombia, where this one was photographed.

PLATE *29*

Black-tailed Tityra

Tityra cayana

RANGE: Tropical zone. Most of South America east of the Andes and south to northeastern Bolivia, Paraguay, and northeastern Argentina.
Length, 8¾ inches

Black-tailed Tityras live in pairs in semiopen habitats, especially burnt-over areas with dead trees or coffee and cocoa plantations. Their light colors, wing-clapping takeoff, and rattling note make them conspicuous as they fly between treetops. They eat fruits and berries. (The bird photographed here was lured down to the level of our mist nets by some ripe Melastome berries.) The Black-tailed Tityra nests in old woodpecker holes high in dead trees. The sexes are similar except for the male's darker gray back. Among other tityras studied, only the female incubates the eggs, but the male helps feed the nestlings.

PLATE *30*

Andean Cock-of-the-rock

Rupicola peruviana

RANGE: Upper tropical and subtropical zones. Venezuela, Colombia,
Ecuador, Peru, and Bolivia.
Length, 14 inches

Cocks-of-the-rock prefer secluded regions in damp forests near
swift mountain streams. Their diet consists of fruit and insects.
The males of the Guianan Cock-of-the-rock—and perhaps the
Andean Cock-of-the-rock as well—engage in elaborate communal
displays within yards of one another. These social displays
involve small defended courting grounds within a larger arena.
The females construct nests of mud and sticks decorated with
moss, which are placed on ledges in caves or on the face of
cliffs over swift streams. Two eggs are laid. The purpose of the
crest which covers the bill of the male is unknown. Perhaps
it has some courtship significance as the female has a very
much reduced crest.

PLATE **31**

Family PIPRIDAE: Manakins

The manakins comprise almost 60 species of active, sparrow-sized birds, all limited to the American tropics. They live on fruits and insects. The males have "courts" or selected perches where they perform an array of elaborate courtship displays showing off their bright colors, accompanied by acrobatics, vocal noises, and wing-snapping sounds. The females, usually dull olive-green in color, do all the work of building the nest and raising the young alone.

Little is known about the Wire-tailed Manakin. Its unusual tail is probably a special feature to attract females during its courtship display. The usual manakin nest is a thin-walled cup hung in the fork of a twig, but the Wire-tailed Manakin constructs a much less tidy nest with excess nesting material hanging down below the cup.

Wire-tailed Manakin

Teleonema filicauda

RANGE: Tropical zone. Northern Venezuela southward east of the
Andes to northeastern Peru and western Brazil.
Length, 5½ inches

63

PLATE *32*

Red-capped Manakins, like others of this family, live largely on fruits but occasionally make quick flights to catch insects. For several months of the year the males spend most of their time on their display perches—slender, horizontal twigs or vines 15 to 50 feet above the ground. Groups of four or five males may have their perches near each other. When a female approaches, the males display vigorously, straightening their legs to expose their yellow thighs and rapidly pivoting 180 degrees on their perches, sidling backwards, or darting to other perches and back again. These movements are accompanied by a variety of whining, snapping calls and clapping noises produced mechanically with the wings.

Red-capped Manakin

Pipra mentalis

RANGE: Tropical and subtropical zone. Southern Mexico through
Central America and west of the Andes south to Ecuador.
Length, 4½ inches

PLATE *33*

The small Striped Manakin possesses a highly developed apparatus for producing mechanical noises—some of the secondary flight feathers are enlarged so that they can produce sound by rattling against each other. In display, two males perch on nearby vertical twigs close to the ground. One flips into a head-downward position and turns rapidly to and fro on the perch. The whirring noises accompanying his movements are thought to be produced by the wing feathers, although during the display it is difficult to tell which noises are vocal and which are mechanical.

Striped Manakin

Machaeropterus regulus

RANGE: Tropical zone. Venezuela south through Colombia, eastern
Ecuador, northeastern Peru, and western Brazil.
Length, 4 inches

PLATE **34**

Family TYRANNIDAE: Tyrant-flycatchers

The tyrant-flycatchers make up the largest family of New World birds, with over 360 species. Its members are so diverse and occupy such a wide range of habitats that it is almost impossible to make any statement which applies to all of them. A typical tyrant-flycatcher pursues flying insects, returning to its perch after each catch to eat. Normally well-developed rictal bristles and bills that are wide at the base assist in catching insects. The plumage of both sexes is usually similar.

Fork-tailed Flycatcher

Muscivora tyrannus

RANGE: Tropical to temperate zones. Southern Mexico south through South America to Patagonia.
Length, 15 inches

The Fork-tailed Flycatcher is a common and distinctive species. It perches upright on any object—a tree, bush, telephone wire, or fence post—in open country and savannah and from this vantage point flies out to catch insects. Fork-tailed Flycatchers occur as scattered individuals or in small groups while foraging, but often congregate in large flocks to roost in trees at night. The nest is an exposed cup at the end of a tree branch. The adults will attack any bird of prey, no matter how large. The southernmost species in South America migrate to northern South America and the Caribbean area during the Southern Hemisphere winter.

PLATE *35*

The raised crest of the Royal Flycatcher is one of the most spectacular sights in the bird world. It is erected and its colors exposed when the bird is held in the hand, but in the wild the crest is so seldom raised that no one is sure of its function. This is a flycatcher of the high shrubs and understory of tall forests and forest edges. It is found singly or in pairs, often near water, where its nest hangs on a slender branch or vine over a stream. The nest is unusual for a flycatcher, looking like a long but inconspicuous tangle of fibers caught on the branch. The eggs are laid in an open-sided niche in the center of this hanging mass, which is one to two yards long. The dark color of the eggs and the barred plumage of the juvenile birds are also unusual among flycatchers.

Royal Flycatcher

Onychorhynchus coronatus
Left: crest up   Above: normal
RANGE: Tropical zone. Southern Mexico to northern Colombia and
northwest Venezuela.
Length, 6¾ inches

PLATE **36**

Family CYCLARHIDAE: Peppershrikes

There are only two species of peppershrikes in the world, the Rufous-browed Peppershrike, shown here, and the Black-billed Peppershrike, which is limited to Ecuador and Colombia. Strong hooked and laterally compressed bills distinguish these birds. They feed upon a variety of small animals, mostly insects.

Rufous-browed Peppershrike

Cyclarhis gujanensis

RANGE: Tropical and subtropical zones. Southeastern Mexico through Central America and South America to Bolivia and Argentina. Length, 6½ inches

The Rufous-browed Peppershrike moves slowly and deliberately through vegetation at medium heights in open woodlands, cultivated areas, dry forests, and mangroves, inspecting the foliage for its prey. It holds large food items, such as caterpillars, under its foot and tears off bites. The Rufous-browed Peppershrike sings a rich, mellow, melodious song, which it repeats over and over from the tops of trees and bushes. This species is always found alone or in pairs. Its nest, thin-walled and semipendent, hangs in a fork well off the ground.

PLATE *37*

Family VIREOLANIIDAE: Shrike-vireos

The three or four species of shrike-vireos are restricted to the American tropics. They show a close affinity to the vireos and are sometimes placed in the vireo family. The bill of a shrike-vireo is heavier and more hooked at the tip than a vireo's bill. One species occurs in oak forests in southern Mexico and Guatemala. The others live in the rain forests of Central and South America. All are inconspicuous, solitary birds of the treetops and little is known about them.

The Slaty-capped Shrike-vireo moves slowly and deliberately, gleaning insects from leaves in the canopy and understory of heavy or second-growth forests. It was unusual that the individual in this photograph came low enough to be caught in our nets. It behaved strangely in the enclosure, peering intently first in one direction, then another, as if studying its surroundings.

Slaty-capped Shrike-vireo

Smaragdolanius leucotis

RANGE: Tropical and subtropical zones. Northern South America south
to Brazil and Bolivia.
Length, 6¼ inches

PLATE **38**

Family ICTERIDAE: Orioles

The 94 species of orioles occur only in the Western Hemisphere, where they are most abundant in the tropics. Orioles are typically medium-sized birds with long wings, strong legs and feet, and hard, pointed bills. They are strong fliers, and many migrate great distances. Most are gregarious, and many of them nest in colonies. Their food preferences are varied—all eat insects and most eat seeds and grain. Many of the tropical species are fruit eaters.

The Oriole Blackbird frequents gardens, fields, and open woodland, walking about over open ground and perching on posts and other low elevations. When alarmed, it flies up into the trees. In flight, the black feet show distinctly against the clear yellow of the abdomen. The Oriole Blackbird eats both fruits and insects; flocks of this species sometimes greatly damage ripening fruit crops. It builds a bulky cup-shaped nest in which it deposits three pale blue eggs. The sexes are similar.

Oriole Blackbird

Gymnomystax mexicanus

RANGE: Tropical zone. The Guianas, Venezuela, Colombia, Ecuador,
Peru, and Brazil.
Length, 11 inches

77

PLATE **39**

Family COEREBIDAE: Honeycreepers

The 37 species of American honeycreepers form several groups of birds which vary widely—so much so that some taxonomists feel that some groups have descended from tanagers, others from wood warbler stock, and that therefore they should not all be in the same family. They are not related to the Hawaiian honeycreepers. Their bills are developed for various methods of obtaining nectar from flowers, but apparently all of them also eat insects at times.

There are seven species in the conebill group, which, as their name implies, have straight, cone-shaped bills. We located a few Blue-backed Conebills in one area in the temperate zone of the Central Andes, but our experience indicates that they are quite uncommon in the Colombian part of their range. They inhabit forests at middle to high elevations in the Andes.

Blue-backed Conebill

Conirostrum sitticolor

RANGE: Subtropical and temperate zones. Venezuela, Colombia,
Ecuador, Peru, and Bolivia.
Length, 5½ inches

PLATE **40**

The flower-piercers feed in a very special way. The sharply hooked upper mandible is hooked over the corolla tube of a flower to prevent it from slipping away, and the short, upwardly tilted lower mandible pierces the corolla. Then the tongue is inserted into the perforation to suck out the nectar. This operation is performed rapidly, enabling the bird to visit many flowers and gather much nectar in a very short time. Flower-piercers also catch insects on the wing. Unlike other honeycreepers, flower-piercers frequent low, bushy growth rather than treetops. The Indigo Flower-piercer pictured is perched on the stalk of a Bromeliad.

Indigo Flower-piercer

Diglossa indigotica

RANGE: Upper tropical and subtropical zones. Colombia and Ecuador.
Length, 4½ inches

PLATE *41*

Purple Honeycreeper

Cyanerpes caeruleus

Above: male   Below: female

RANGE: Tropical zone. The Guianas, Venezuela, Colombia, Ecuador, Peru, Brazil, and Bolivia.
Length, 4½ inches

The Purple Honeycreeper travels in groups, generally keeping to the tops of tall flowering trees. It feeds on nectar and fruit—it is especially fond of overripe oranges—and captures insects on the wing. The cup-shaped nest contains two white eggs with violet and maroon spotting.

PLATE *42*

The Red-legged Honeycreeper is generally encountered in small flocks that work their way through trees along forest borders or in open, thinned, or scrubby woodland. It probes flowers of diverse kinds, apparently using its long slender bill and protrusible tongue to suck up nectar or capture insects inside the blossom. It creeps along branches in tanager fashion, often hanging head downward. It also catches insects on the wing and is fond of ripe bananas. The small cuplike nest is built by the female alone. Unlike other tropical passerine birds, the males change into a duller plumage after the breeding season.

Red-legged Honeycreeper

Cyanerpes cyaneus

RANGE: Tropical zone. Southern Mexico south to Brazil, Peru, and
Bolivia; Cuba.
Length, 5 inches

PLATE *43*

Family TERSINIDAE:
The Swallow-tanager

Superficially the peculiar Swallow-tanager resembles a tanager, but its graceful and rapid flight when taking insects on the wing is similar to that of a swallow. In structure and behavior, however, it is so unusual that it has been placed in a separate family. The Swallow-tanager, a bird of the open woodlands, feeds on fruit as well as insects. The song, which is frequently given, is shrill and metallic. A favorite perch is among the topmost bare twigs of a tall tree. This species is partially migratory, breeding in the mountains but at other seasons gathering in large flocks in the lower regions. It nests in stone walls, cliffs, or earthen banks in which the female excavates a tunnel.

Swallow-tanager

Tersina viridis

RANGE: Tropical and lower subtropical zones. Panama south to
northern Argentina, Paraguay, and southern Brazil.
Length, 5½ inches

PLATE 44

Family THRAUPIDAE: Tanagers

Tanagers make up a large, exclusively New World family of small to medium-sized birds of varied appearance and habits, notable for their brilliant colors. They present many problems to the taxonomist, showing strong similarities to both the finches and the wood warblers. One taxonomic feature that characterizes most species of tanagers is the notch near the end of the upper mandible. Except for the four species occurring north of Mexico, tanagers are nonmigratory, although some species of the Central and South American highlands wander altitudinally with the seasons. With the exception of the thrush-tanager, their voices are poorly developed, and the majority of species have either weak songs and whistles or no songs at all. They subsist largely on fruit.

The Fawn-breasted Tanager prefers bushy pastures and forest edges. Despite its wide range, no studies have been made of its habits. We caught this bird quite close to the ground at a small berry bush, not over five feet high.

Fawn-breasted Tanager

Pipraeidea melanonota

RANGE: Upper tropical to lower temperate zone. Colombia and Venezuela south to Bolivia; eastern Brazil south to Uruguay, Paraguay, and Argentina.
Length, 6 inches

PLATE **45**

The beautiful and brightly colored Glistening-green Tanager lives only in the mountain forests of its small range. These forests are being cut down so fast that its survival is in considerable doubt. Its habits have not been studied. The plant in the picture is *Anthurium lactiflorum*. I did not observe the bird eating its berries.

Glistening-green Tanager

Chlorochrysa phoenicotis

RANGE: Upper tropical and lower subtropical zone. Colombia and
Ecuador.
Length, 5½ inches

PLATE *46*

Multicolored Tanager

Chlorochrysa nitidissima

RANGE: Upper tropical and subtropical zone. Colombia.
Length, 5 inches

The variety of vivid colors on the small Multicolored Tanager
is almost unbelievable—this is certainly among the most
colorful birds in the world. The Multicolored Tanager is
limited to a small area of the mountains in southwestern
Colombia. It faces a very dim future, for the forests are being
cut and burned to feed a swiftly expanding population.

PLATE **47**

In Spanish the Paradise Tanager, an extraordinarily colorful bird, is known as *siete colores* (seven colors). Although the Indians hunt it to use its feathers as ornaments, this hunting has not greatly affected its numbers over the years, and it is still fairly common in some areas. The sexes are similar. No information has been obtained on nesting habits.

Paradise Tanager

Tangara chilensis

RANGE: Tropical zone. The Guianas, Venezuela, Colombia, Ecuador,
Peru, Bolivia, and Brazil.
Length, 6 inches

PLATE *48*

The Green-and-gold Tanager is an uncommon resident of the forests of the Amazon basin east of the Andes and west of the Andes in Colombia. This specimen, the only one we observed, had joined a flock of other birds to feed on the newly ripened berries of the Melastome bush shown. Its life history is unknown.

Green-and-gold Tanager

Tangara schrankii

RANGE: Tropical zone. Venezuela, Colombia, Ecuador, Peru, Brazil, and Bolivia.
Length, 5 inches

PLATE *49*

Fairly common in the humid forests of its range, the small,
brightly colored Emerald Tanager is often found in the
company of other foraging birds of the same genus. It has
not been studied and practically nothing is known of its
habits, but we did observe that it tended to stay high above
the ground in the crowns of the trees.

Emerald Tanager

Tangara florida

RANGE: Tropical and lower subtropical zones. Costa Rica through Panama and along the Pacific coast of Colombia.
Length, 5 inches

PLATE **50**

The bright yellow of the Golden Tanager stands out in the darkest of the humid forests where it lives. We often observed it traveling with a fairly large flock of other birds of many kinds, searching along moss-covered limbs as if for insects. Its breeding and nesting habits have not been recorded.

Golden Tanager

Tangara arthus

RANGE: Upper tropical and subtropical zones of Colombia, Venezuela,
Ecuador, Peru and Bolivia.
Length, 5 inches

PLATE **51**

Second-growth woodland and brushy pastures are the preferred habitat of the Blue-necked Tanager. Such areas commonly result from the clearing of the forest, and birds which have adapted to such places seem to have a much more secure future than those dependent on forest. The bird pictured is perched on a Melastome, the berries of which are among its favorite foods.

Blue-necked Tanager

Tangara cyanicollis

RANGE: Upper tropical and lower subtropical zones. Venezuela,
Colombia, Ecuador, Brazil, Peru, and Bolivia.
Length, 5½ inches

PLATE **52**

The Bay-headed Tanager is found in forests and open land at the edge of forests. Its diet is a variety of fruits and insects. This tanager is a somewhat better songster than its near relatives. The male's song consists of four or five notes descending in pitch, delivered with a whining twang. The nest is a fairly bulky open cup made of moss, bamboo leaves, fungal filaments, and other such materials. The male helps a little in nest building at the beginning but soon loses interest. The nestlings are fed by both parents. When they leave the nest, the young are dull green in plumage—they acquire their bright colors in a postjuvenal molt.

Bay-headed Tanager

Tangara gyrola

RANGE: Tropical and lower subtropical zones. Costa Rica south to Colombia, Venezuela, the Guianas, Brazil, Ecuador, Peru, and Bolivia. Length, 5½ inches

PLATE *53*

The Blue-and-black Tanager is a bird of forest and scrub at
middle to higher elevations in the Andes Mountains. Though
normally a forest bird, we found it in a number of cutover
areas with no real forest nearby. Its feeding and nesting
habits have not yet been studied.

Blue-and-black Tanager

Tangara vassorii

RANGE: Subtropical and temperate zones. Venezuela, Colombia,
Ecuador, Peru, and Bolivia.
Length, 5½ inches

PLATE *54*

Humid, cool forests are the preference of the Yellow-throated
Tanager. We found small populations of this species in
only two areas of Colombia. There are undoubtedly others,
but we can safely say that it is uncommon throughout
most of its range. Its habits are not known.

Yellow-throated Tanager

Iridosornis analis

RANGE: Upper tropical and subtropical zones. Colombia, Ecuador,
Peru, and Bolivia.
Length, 6 inches

PLATE 55

Although the literature states that the Golden-crowned Tanager prefers humid forests in the temperate zone of the Andes, we found it fairly common in several areas with shrubs and low trees at higher elevations of the mountains. Despite its appeal because of its strikingly beautiful colors, no study has been made of its habits.

Golden-crowned Tanager

Iridosornis rufivertex

RANGE: Temperate zone. Venezuela, Colombia, and Ecuador.
Length, 7 inches

PLATE *56*

The Scarlet-bellied Mountain-tanager lives in the higher regions of the Andes, where it is found in both forested and semiopen areas. Nothing is recorded of its habits.

Scarlet-bellied Mountain-tanager

Anisognathus igniventris

RANGE: Upper subtropical to temperate zones. Venezuela, Colombia, Ecuador, Peru, and Bolivia. Length, 7½ inches

PLATE 57

The Blue-winged Mountain-tanager is a forest species. We found it common in one area near Cali, Colombia, but absent in the other sections of its range that we visited. This bird soon calmed down in the enclosure. We offered it berries of *Psychotria parasitica*, as shown, which it mashed in its beak, extracting the juice and then discarding the pulp.

Blue-winged Mountain-tanager

Anisognathus flavinucha

RANGE: Subtropical zone. Venezuela, Colombia, Ecuador, Peru, and
Bolivia.
Length, 7 inches

PLATE *58*

Hooded Mountain-tanager

Buthraupis montana

RANGE: Subtropical and temperate zones. Venezuela, Colombia, Ecuador, Peru, and Bolivia.
Length, 10 inches

The Hooded Mountain-tanager is one of the largest of the tanagers. It lives in heavily forested areas and is probably dependent on such areas for its survival, as we never found it where big trees were absent. Its habits are not known.

PLATE *59*

Moss-backed Tanager

Bangsia edwardsi

RANGE: Tropical and lower subtropical zones. Colombia and Ecuador.
Length, 6½ inches

Many tanagers seem to flout the usual ideas about
camouflage, but the coloration of the Moss-backed Tanager
makes it quite inconspicuous on the moss-covered limbs
in the humid forests of its limited range. Nothing has
been recorded of its habits.

PLATE 60

The Crimson-backed Tanager is found more often in clearings and open country than in heavy forests. Although it sometimes sits on high, exposed perches, where its brilliant scarlet back attracts the eye from a distance of several hundred feet, it is usually found in family groups in bushes or low trees. This tanager is active and hard to approach. It has a distinctive sharp alarm call. The male takes no part in nest building, incubating, or brooding, although it does help in feeding the young. Unlike many other tanagers, however, males of the *Ramphocelus* genus do not feed the female on the nest.

Crimson-backed Tanager

Ramphocelus dimidiatus

RANGE: Tropical zone. Panama, Colombia, and Venezuela.
Length, 7 inches

PLATE **61**

The Masked Crimson Tanager prefers a well-forested area and is much less common than its close relative, the Crimson-backed Tanager (Plate 60). We obtained this male Masked Crimson Tanager to photograph when one of his young flew into a net. The parent birds were nearby but were too wary to get caught. As we removed the young bird from the net and held it, the parents dove at us. Seeing this, we concealed ourselves near another net. The young bird's calls lured the parents down and soon they both were also caught. After the photography, we released them all together.

Masked Crimson Tanager

Ramphocelus nigrogularis

RANGE: Tropical zone. Colombia, Ecuador, Peru, and Brazil.
Length, 7½ inches

123

PLATE *62*

Yellow-rumped Tanager

Ramphocelus icteronotus

RANGE: Tropical and subtropical zones. Panama, Colombia, and
Ecuador.
Length, 8 inches

The Yellow-rumped Tanager prefers clearings, brushland,
and scrubby woodland, especially along the banks of
rivers and streams. It is highly gregarious and during
the nonbreeding season is usually encountered in groups
of up to 10 or 12 individuals. It is semicolonial in
nesting habits; the males defend individual territories
during breeding, but these territories are often small
and crowded together in clusters. This restless and noisy
bird has a variety of calls and notes which may be nasal,
rattling, or quite melodious. We found it common in
Panama but much less so in Colombia.

PLATE *63*

Although anatomical studies place the Rose-breasted Thrush-tanager with the tanagers, it is a ground feeder like a thrasher and sings more like a wren. Further study may show that it belongs in another family. This species is almost always found in pairs, which sing antiphonally during courtship. The male helps in incubating the eggs as well as in other nesting duties. They are difficult to observe for they prefer dense thickets. They are apparently entirely insectivorous.

Rose-breasted Thrush-tanager

Rhodinocichla rosea

RANGE: Upper tropical and lower subtropical zones. Western Mexico
and Costa Rica south to Colombia and Venezuela.
Length, 8 inches

PLATE **64**

The brilliant Scarlet-and-white Tanager must now be quite rare—we spent a number of weeks in its area and were able to get only this one male to photograph. His flaming red color catches the eye immediately in the forest. The female is a dull olive brown. They live in secondary growth, open forest, and forest borders, but otherwise their habits have not been recorded.

Scarlet-and-white Tanager

Erythrothlypis salmoni

RANGE: Tropical zone. Colombia and Ecuador.
Length, 5½ inches

PLATE 65

There are nine species of the *Hemispingus* genus in the
tropics. In their small bill and plumage pattern they
resemble some of the members of the wood warbler family.
Ornithologists are not in complete agreement about where
they belong. The Black-capped Hemispingus is a forest bird
of middle altitudes. In this photograph it is perched on
an emerging frond of a tree fern, a plant that often grows
to a height of 20 to 30 feet in the rain forest.

Black-capped Hemispingus

Hemispingus atropileus

RANGE: Tropical and temperate zones. Venezuela, Colombia, Ecuador,
Peru, and Bolivia.
Length, 6¾ inches

PLATE 66

Grass-green Tanager

Chlorornis riefferii

RANGE: Upper tropical to temperate zones. Colombia, Ecuador,
Peru, and Bolivia.
Length, 8½ inches

The Grass-green Tanager lives in forests at middle
altitudes in the Andes. Unlike most of the tanagers,
its color makes it inconspicuous among the foliage.
We usually found this tanager in mixed flocks of several
species. These loose flocks of feeding birds—sometimes
quite large, covering several acres—move slowly through
the trees. After a flock has passed, the forest seems quite
devoid of birds until the next flock comes. The Grass-green
Tanager has not been studied and little is known of its habits.

PLATE *67*

A medium-sized, long-tailed bird showing much white when flying is likely to be the Magpie Tanager. It has a plumage unlike that of any of its relatives—the pointed black breast feathers are particularly distinctive. It is seen in small bands in second growth and brushy areas. Its habits are rather jaylike. The sexes are similar.

Magpie Tanager

Cissopis leveriana

RANGE: Tropical and subtropical zones. Venezuela, the Guianas,
Colombia, Ecuador, Peru, Brazil, Bolivia, and Argentina.
Length, 11 inches

PLATE **68**

Family CATAMBLYRHYNCHIDAE:
The Plush-capped Finch

The Plush-capped Finch is named for the dense patch of short, velvety feathers on the forehead. It is the only member of its family, though further study may place it with the tanagers or the finches. This uncommon and little-known bird is found in open woodland and sparsely wooded country of the high Andes, usually in isolated pairs or mingled with flocks of other birds.

Plush-capped Finch

Catamblyrhynchus diadema

RANGE: Subtropical to temperate zones. Venezuela, Colombia,
Ecuador, Peru, Bolivia, and Argentina.
Length, 5½ inches

PLATE **69**

Family FRINGILLIDAE: Finches

Finches constitute a very large and complex family of small birds found throughout most of the world. In contrast to tanagers, most finches are of dull plumage, although a few species are brilliantly colored. The majority of finches, however, have a well-developed and pleasing song, which they usually give from a perch, rarely in flight. Their short, conical, pointed bills are adapted principally for seed eating. They forage mostly on or near the ground. Almost all of them are strong fliers, and many species outside the tropics are migratory.

The Pileated Finch is a bird of thickets and scrub in arid tropical areas. It feeds on the ground. In flight, the black of the wings and tail contrasts with the gray and white of the body plumage. The female lacks the crest, which in the male is normally flattened down and semiconcealed. The nest is hemispherical and placed under low vegetation. The eggs—usually there are three—are white.

Pileated Finch

Coryphospingus pileatus

RANGE: Tropical zone. Venezuela, Colombia, and Brazil.
Length, 5½ inches

PLATE *70*

Owing to their habit of lurking on or near the ground in brushy thickets, finches of the genus *Atlapetes* are known as brush-finches. Whereas other ground-feeding finches scratch dead leaves aside by kicking with their feet, the brush-finches flick them away with sideswipes of the bill. The food of the Ochre-breasted Brush-finch is apparently made up largely of small invertebrates, but since they have not been studied, little is really known about them.

Ochre-breasted Brush-finch

Atlapetes semirufus

RANGE: Subtropical to temperate zones. Venezuela and Colombia.
Length, 7 inches

PLATE *71*

Until recently, the Tanager-finch was considered to be a tanager instead of a finch. Anatomically it has features of both families. One observer reports that it is a terrestrial bird, usually scratching in the ground litter like a finch. More study of its habits should provide the answer. This rare species is restricted to a small area of the western Andes.

Tanager-finch

Oreothraupis arremonops

RANGE: Upper subtropical zone. Colombia and Ecuador.
Length, 9 inches

PLATE *72*

The widely distributed Orange-billed Sparrow is a shy bird of the moist forest floor, often found near streams or ravines. It forages in the damp ground litter or in low, dense cover and tangles, rarely rising more than 10 feet above the ground. Its food is made up mostly of insects. The song, which is delivered from the ground, a fallen log, or a low perch, consists usually of five very high-pitched, soft notes. The Orange-billed Sparrow nests on the ground, usually against a slope of some sort. The nest is a bulky, roofed-over oven-shaped structure with an elevated entrance facing down the slope. Two eggs are laid. The female alone incubates and broods, but the male plays a major role in feeding the nestlings.

Orange-billed Sparrow

Arremon aurantiirostris

RANGE: Tropical zone. Southern Mexico through Panama to Colombia,
Ecuador, and Peru.
Length, 6½ inches

Methods and Equipment

CLOSE-UP photography of any moving object such as a bird involves two basic problems—getting enough light and sharp focus. Under tropical forest conditions it is extremely difficult, in many cases almost impossible, to solve these problems by the normal method: setting up camera and lights at some spot to which the bird will come. Many tropical forest birds spend most of their time in the treetops, up to 100 or more feet above the ground. At lower levels of the forest, reliable sunlight ("available light") is almost nonexistent. So we solve these problems by creating our own light with electronic stroboscopic flash and bringing the bird to the lights and camera, all set up in advance in an enclosure.

The bird is captured in a mist net, some 40 feet long and 10 feet high, constructed of very fine black nylon thread, which is practically invisible. After being carefully released, the bird is put in a cloth bag which gives sufficient air, yet is dark enough to keep the bird fairly quiet.

The next task is to mount the proper perch and fresh foliage in the enclosure. We try to use foliage similar to that which we have observed the birds using in the wild. If the subject's natural food is known and available, it helps to put some in the enclosure.

If quiet is maintained after the bird is put in the enclosure, it usually soon calms down and rests on the perch, if it is a properly chosen one. Often within half an hour the photography has

SKETCH OF ENCLOSURE
(not to scale)

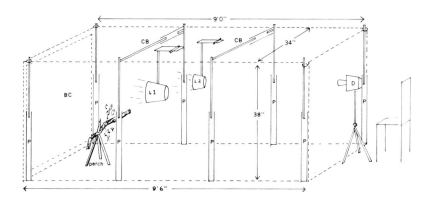

CROSS BRACE
2 needed

thumbscrew · 7/16 x 1½" tubing welded on bar

open end

|← 18" →| |← 25" →|

POST
8 needed

BACKGROUND FRAME SIDE
4 needed

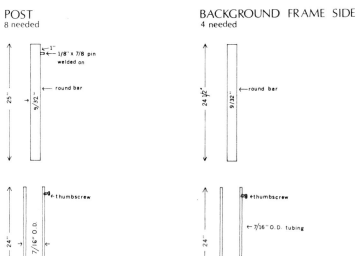

1"
1/8" x 7/8 pin welded on
9/32"
← round bar
25"

thumbscrew →
7/16" O.D.
24"
bottom made watertight by welding

24½"
9/32"
← round bar

←thumbscrew
← 7/16" O.D. tubing
24"
← thumbscrew
|← 2" →|

been completed and the bird is released unharmed in its own home area.

In the accompanying sketch, the enclosure is made of fairly heavy unbleached white muslin. This provides enough light inside for focusing but keeps the birds from seeing through it. Four collapsible poles (P) along each side, with two cross braces (CB) across the middle ones, hold the enclosure up, and it becomes quite firm and rigid when the four corners are tied to convenient trees or to stakes. There is a skirt, about 12 inches wide all around, to accommodate unevenness in the ground. It is weighted down with sticks or stones to prevent the bird's escape under the enclosure.

Eight loops—one at each corner of the enclosure and two on two opposite sides—slip over the tops of the eight poles to hold the enclosure up. To prevent each loop from slipping down the pole, a 1/8-inch pin is welded on the top section of the pole about 1 inch from the end.

There is a zippered opening at one end of the enclosure through which only the lens of the camera (D) is inserted, so that all operating parts of the camera are outside the enclosure. The camera is always mounted on a tripod. There are also zippers (not shown in the sketch) in the sides, for putting in the perches and background foliage, and in the top, for inserting the lights and the background cloth.

The strobe main light (L_1) and the fill light (L_2) are suspended from the canvas top of the enclosure through zippered openings. Flashbulbs could be used, but I have found strobes more useful. The light aluminum bars holding the lights are slipped through safety pins in the top of the enclosure to keep them positioned. The two lights must be kept far enough to the sides to avoid throwing a shadow on the background cloth, but within this limitation, the angle and distance of the lights can be varied to produce a variety of pleasing results. The addition of a backlight sometimes works well, too, though of course every added light cuts the intensity of the main light, thus giving less depth of field.

The eight poles are constructed of 7/16-inch (outside diameter) aluminum tubing, into which a 9/32-inch round aluminum bar slides. These poles, when collapsed to their shortest length, will just fit into a 26-inch suitcase for traveling. A thumbscrew (1/4-inch × 20 thread) on the tubing can be tightened to hold the inner rod at any position, thus making the poles the right length to suit ground conditions. This is made by putting a 1/4-inch × 20 aluminum nut on the thumbscrew and peening the end threads of the thumbscrew with a hammer, so that the nut cannot come off. A 9/32-inch hole is then drilled in the tubing approximately 3/4 inch from one end. The end of the thumbscrew is inserted in this hole and the aluminum nut on the thumbscrew is welded to the tubing. The bottom end of the tubing is welded tight to keep water and dirt from getting in.

The two cross braces are constructed of 7/16-inch aluminum tubing into which a 9/32-inch aluminum bar slides. A thumbscrew is welded to the tubing 3/4 inch from one end. The other end of the tubing is left open. A short piece of 7/16-inch aluminum tubing is welded on one end of the 9/32-inch aluminum bar. The two ends of the cross brace are slipped over the 1/8-inch

Enclosure erected in tropics, under canopy used to keep off sun and rain

pins on the poles. The cross brace is then extended until the top of the enclosure is firm and the thumbscrew is tightened.

The background cloth (BC) is stretched over a background frame formed of the same sizes of aluminum as the poles (see sketch). The four sides of the background frame fit together to make a rectangle over which the background cloth is stretched. The corners of the background cloth are sewn to form a pocket into which the frame fits. Then the background frame is expanded to make the background cloth tight, and the four thumbscrews are tightened to hold it there. The background cloth on the background frame is inserted inside the enclosure through a wide zipper (not shown in sketch) on the top of the enclosure at the back. It helps keep the cloth clean if it is tilted inward at the top about 6 inches. To allow for this, the enclosure is made 6 inches longer at the bottom than at the top.

The background cloths have been the subject of much experimenting. In general we think a light blue color gives the best results, but individual preference may govern that. Many of the newer synthetic fabrics look one color in daylight but photograph a different color. The background cloth is dampened thoroughly before being put on the frame to remove all wrinkles which would show in the picture. Of course spare cloths are needed, as they get soiled quickly.

Mounting the perch and background foliage inside the enclosure has to be worked out for each setup. Sometimes the perch is stuck into the ground, sometimes it is suspended from the top of the enclosure. I have found a low tripod with a Kodapod clamp invaluable. It is important to have the perch far enough away from the background cloth so that shadows do not show on the cloth.

Selecting the proper perch for the bird is a matter which often requires much trial and error. I have frequently had a bird refuse to land on a perch, then after I have changed the perch, pose almost immediately.

After the film has been exposed, I find it important to store it in a plastic bag with one or two containers of silica gel to keep it dry.

Most film manufacturers advise development soon after exposure, but I have had no trouble keeping film up to six or eight weeks after exposure, provided it is kept dry and not overheated.

I have presented the details of my technique here solely as a guide. I am sure many variations could be used which would serve equally well—perhaps better. I hope many of my readers will work out their own methods. It is a lot of fun!

References

AUSTIN, OLIVER L., JR. *Birds of the World*. Golden Press, 1961.

EISENMANN, EUGENE. *The Species of Middle American Birds*. Linnaean Society of New York, 1955.

FISHER, JAMES, AND ROGER T. PETERSON. *The World of Birds*. Doubleday, 1968.

HAVERSCHMIDT, FRANCOIS. *The Birds of Surinam*. Livingston, 1968.

MEYER DE SCHAUENSEE, R. *Birds of Colombia*. Livingston, 1964.

_____. *The Species of Birds of South America and Their Distribution*. Livingston, 1966.

MONROE, BURT L., JR. *A Distributional Survey of the Birds of Honduras*. American Ornithologists Union Monograph No. 7, 1968.

RUSSELL, STEPHEN M. *A Distributional Study of the Birds of British Honduras*. American Ornithologists Union Monograph No. 1, 1964.

SKUTCH, ALEXANDER F. *Life Histories of Central American Birds*. Cooper Ornithological Society, Berkeley, Cal. Vol. I, 1954; Vol. II, 1960.

SLUD, PAUL. *The Birds of Costa Rica*. A Bulletin of the American Museum of Natural History. Vol. 128, 1964.

SMITHE, FRANK B. *The Birds of Tikal*. Natural History Press, 1966.

THOMSON, A. LANDSBOROUGH, ED. *A New Dictionary of Birds*. McGraw-Hill, 1964.

WETMORE, ALEXANDER. *Birds of the Republic of Panama*. Random House, 1968.

Printed by Smeets Lithographers, Weert
Bound by Proost en Brandt, Amsterdam
Typography by Alfred B. Carson Typography,
Broomall, Pa.